Rule for a
New Brother

Paul,

May this little book enrich
your life as you work, study,
pray, and serve to the
Glory of our awesome God.

Always in the love which
has first been given to us,

Ami

Rule for a New Brother

By H. van der Looy

Wood engravings by Adé Bethune
Foreword by Henri J. M. Nouwen

TEMPLEGATE PUBLISHERS
Springfield, Illinois

First published in Great Britain in 1973 by
Darton, Longman & Todd Limited
89 Lillie Road, London SW6 1UD
© 1973 Benedictine Priory 'Regina Pacis'

Regel voor een nieuwe broeder
by the Brakkenstein Community of
Blessed Sacrament Fathers, Holland
English translation by the
Benedictine Nuns of Cockfosters
Reprinted 1974 and 1975

U.S. edition © 1976
Reprinted 1977, 1978, 1979, 1980, 1982, 1985
New edition with foreword by
Henri J. M. Nouwen © 1987
Templegate Publishers
302 East Adams Street, P.O. Box 5152
Springfield, Illinois 62705
ISBN 0-87243-165-7

The translators thank Fr. James Dekker, S.S.S.,
for his kindness in putting his own translation of
the original at their disposal; Mrs. Rosemary
Haughton and Dom Barnabas Sandeman, O.S.B.,
for their advice on style; and the author, Fr. Dr.
H. van der Looy of Brakkenstein, for his
generous help and patience with the translation.

Table of Contents

Foreword by Henri J. M. Nouwen 7
1. Seeking God 17
2. Following Jesus 22
3. Members of One Body 26
4. For the Sake of the Kingdom . . . 36
5. Called to Freedom 41
6. That We Might Be Rich 46
7. The Breaking of the Bread 52
8. Prayer 60
9. The Harvest is Great 66
10. The Body of the Lord 74
11. The Spiritual Life 79
12. Mary 87
13. Of Days and Years 89
14. The End and the Beginning 93

Foreword

This is a rule. Not a rule that restricts freedom but a rule that wants to offer freedom. It is a rule first of all written for men who desire to enter into a religious community. But since it offers ways to find the freedom to love, I can hardly imagine that there is any man or woman who will not find in these pages something that speaks to the searching heart. It is a rule written for people who are considering living and working in a community supported by vows of chastity, obedience and poverty. But since these vows emerge from a desire to belong completely to God, there is no human being who cannot find true spiritual counsel here. It is a rule written for Catholics, but since it finds its inspiration in God's all-inclusive mercy, every person who desires to live an upright life will find invaluable treasures in it.

I have read this rule many times and even though I do not consider entering a religious order, I keep finding here many words that help me in my struggle to live a faithful life. That is because this rule wants to teach the heart to love. Love is not the only response of the human heart. The heart can also fear, hate, brood, be resentful and contemplate revenge. For the heart to respond spontaneously in love it needs to be taught by love. The author says to the new brother: 'You are someone only in so far as you are love, and only what has turned to love in your life will be preserved.' Turning everything to love; that is what this rule is all about. Or maybe I should say: letting everything be turned into love; because what this little book shows most clearly is that the freedom to love, which is the goal of the spiritual life, is not the result of complicated human strategies or techniques, but the fruit of God's work in us.

Here the deeper meaning of any rule in the spiritual life becomes visible. Instead of giving us methods to control, direct and determine our own life, a spiritual rule wants to offer an open and free space within and among us where God can touch us with God's loving presence. It wants to make it possible for us not so much to find God as to be found by God, not so much to direct our life towards God, as to be directed by God, not so much to love God as to be loved by God.

This might sound quite passive. But the contrary is true. It requires active spiritual work to keep space for God. Why? Our ever-present fears keep trying to fill up every bit of free space with countless thoughts, words and actions that can give us the illusion that after all *we* are in control. Even though we have learned the hard way how little in control we really are, and even though we continue to suffer from the consequences of a life built on illusion, it remains very difficult to let God be the director and guide of our lives.

The more I think about this the less surprised I am at our human resistance to let God be the Lord of our lives.

Because God is a jealous lover (see 2 Corinthians 11:2) who wants to love every part of us with a divine love and wants to touch every one of our thoughts, words and actions, God is not content with a divided love in which we reserve parts of ourselves for ourselves or others. God does not want to be excluded from any corner of our heart. God wants the divine love to pervade every fibre of our being.

But we hesitate because such a lover might radically change us and lead us where we 'would rather not go' (John 21:18). There are enough stories to give credibility to our hesitation. When Abram let God love him he became Abraham, a new person, being led to unknown places. When Simon let God love him, he became Peter, a new person, being sent out into the wide world and ending his life on a cross. When Saul let God love him he became Paul, a new person, persecuted, often put in prison, finally brought captive to Rome and beheaded there. And still . . . these men and many other men and women who let God love them with a jealous love all found true freedom, a freedom to love. It is for this new-found spiritual freedom that we remember them and continue to celebrate their lives.

A rule in the spiritual life, thus, is a way to create a space where God's jealous love can reach us, heal us, transform us and guide us to freedom even when the cost of that freedom is high. There have been many rules over the centuries: the rule of St Augustine, the rule of St

Benedict, the rule of St Francis, the rule of Taizé, and many others. They differ according to the historical context in which they are written, the people they address and the way of life they envisage. But all of them offer creative boundaries within which God's loving presence can be recognised and celebrated.

The 'Rule for a New Brother' is a contemporary expression of this need for boundaries. In a very compassionate tone it calls us to a discipline of the heart and shows concrete ways in which we can become disciples of Jesus who reveals to us God's jealous love. It does not prescribe but invite, it does not force but guide, it does not threaten but warn, it does not instill fear but points to love. It presents a demanding way of life, but the demands do not come from an outer power that wants to control life but from an inner voice that calls to freedom. In everything it wants to help us to become gradually free from the compulsions of our society so that we can fully belong to God.

This rule speaks about the community as the first place where we can be found and loved by God. In no way does it encourage a form of individual spiritual heroism. All through, the community is presented as the fertile ground for a spiritual life. This community makes its true nature manifest in the celebration of the Eucharist. The bread and wine, taken in small amounts, reveal the presence of a love greater than our hearts can contain and our minds can understand.

In the context of such a eucharistic community chastity, obedience and poverty are ways to deepen our sense of fully belonging to God. The manner in which these three ways of following Jesus are described make it clear that, though they are presented as religious vows, they are also aspects of the life of every Christian. All Christians are called to witness for a love greater than human beings can give each other. All Christians are called to listen to an authoritative voice and all Christians are called to detach themselves from whatever blocks their way to God. Chastity, obedience and poverty are ways of creating in us an inner sanctuary unoccupied by human concerns, kept free for God to dwell in.

The more we belong to God the better we can live a life of prayer and ministry. Prayer is listening to the voice of the lover inviting us to risk a new step in an unknown direction. Ministry is giving visibility to the presence of a loving God inside as well as outside our community of faith.

Finally the rule calls us to love the Church as the Lord himself, and asks for a profound respect for her institutions and missions. A life of prayer and ministry can only bear fruit when it is deeply connected with the whole body of Christ and lived in filial communion with its spiritual leaders. Although the Church is made up of sinners and 'burdened with weakness' she continues to be the place God has chosen to meet us. When we cannot truly love this broken, suffering and often sick body of the Church we have no reason to believe that we are allowing God to reach us. In a very beautiful way the author of the rule says: 'Whatever is impure and useless in the Church must be healed, not attacked, and purified in suffering rather than criticised.' Thus a deep love for the Church in its concrete daily life is a criterion of our deep desire to be found, known and loved by God.

It is no surprise that the author at the conclusion of his rule asks us to look at Mary, the mother of Jesus, as the model of the spiritual life. She, more than any other human being, made space for God and let her whole being be formed by God's zealous love. Her trust and fidelity offer us an example but also encouragement in our own daily struggle to be faithful. She prevents us from becoming angry when the Church does not respond to our need and from becoming bitter when the Church leaves us dissatisfied. She keeps asking our attention for the suffering body of her Son and inviting us to an unceasing willingness to forgive. She safeguards our religion from becoming an ideology and reminds us over and over again that it is Jesus who is the source of all true joy and peace.

We live in a time in which we are constantly tempted to let our fears rule our lives. More than ever our world gives us reasons to fear. We are afraid for our own inner impulses which we are not able fully to understand or control, we are afraid of the many strangers surrounding us and threatening to invade our lives, we are afraid of the increasing capability of humanity to destroy itself and we are afraid of a God who can punish us with eternal damnation. The greater our fears the less our freedom. In order to alleviate our fears we often become very active, busy and full of worries about our future, always on guard for possible dangers. Our fears also make us very self-centred since they make us live our lives as an ongoing battle for survival.

Jesus came to cast out our fears. He announced a God of perfect love in whom no fear can exist. He himself and all his messengers, whether angels or apostles, say constantly: 'Do not be afraid.' But it is far from easy not to let the many real fears make us deaf and blind to the God of perfect love. The news of every day, the concrete emergencies of our own daily life and our own inner self-doubt make us often fearful before we are fully aware of it ourselves.

What we truly need is a safe space to dwell, to take off our heavy armour and let the perfect love of God touch us, heal us and guide us from the land of fear to the land of God.

This rule is one very concrete way of creating such a space. The disciplines it describes can help us gradually to create a new environment with a new familiarity, where we learn to trust our capacity to love more than our inclination to fear. Such a new environment takes time to create. It requires patience and hard spiritual work. But as it is being created we discover that it indeed is possible to live in the midst of this fearful world without being imprisoned by it and that we can already here and now taste the freedom of the children of God, the freedom to love.

HENRI J. M. NOUWEN

1. Seeking God

You want to seek God with all your life,
and love Him with all your heart.

But you would be wrong
if you thought you could reach Him.
Your arms are too short, your eyes are too dim,
your heart and understanding too small.

To seek God
means first of all
to let yourself be found by Him.
He is the God of Abraham, Isaac and Jacob.
He is the God of Jesus Christ.
He is your God,
not because He is yours
but because you are His.

To choose God
is to realise that you are known and loved
in a way surpassing anything one can imagine,
loved before anyone had thought of you
or spoken your name.

To choose God
means giving yourself up to Him in faith.
Let your life be built on this faith
as on an invisible foundation.
Let yourself be carried by this faith
like a child in its mother's womb.

And so,
don't talk too much about God
but live
in the certainty that He has written your name
on the palm of His hand.
Live your human task
in the liberating certainty
that nothing in the world can separate you
from God's love for you.

In Jesus of Nazareth
God shows in a special way
how urgently He seeks for you,
and how entirely He has committed
Himself to your happiness.

In Jesus of Nazareth
one person shows
how completely we can belong to God;
how much freedom and humanity,
how much courage and self-forgetfulness
one can possess
when one has been found by God
and has surrendered to Him.
In Jesus there is also a future for you
as you go by His road through sin and death
towards fellowship and love,
unfailing glory and life.

In faith you will recognize Him
in the works of His hands,

and above all in us,
made in His image and likeness,
and most clearly of all in the love
which is Jesus.

But even if you receive no sign,
no word from Him,
you will still recognize Him.
His very absence
is full of the mystery of his greatness.
It can help you
not to seek and serve some image of Him
you yourself have created.

So never let yourself lose heart
but go on seeking Him
in everything, in everybody -
they are all pledges
that you will finally meet Him.
Work hard to know Him
face to face.

For as sure as the dawn is His coming,
certain as the latter rains.

If you abide in love
you will abide in God
and not wander anymore in darkness.

Then live in joyfulness and hope,
unanxious, without any trace of fear,
at peace with yourself and the world,
in ceaseless reverence and thanks.
Because God's love for you endures forever.

2. Following Jesus

Following Jesus
does not mean slavishly copying His life.
It means making His choice of life your own
starting from your own potential
and in the place where you find yourself.
It means living for the values
for which Jesus lived
and died.

It means following the path He took
and seeing things as He saw them.

If there is anything in which this life,
this way, can be expressed,
in which God has revealed Himself most clearly,
it is the reality of love.
You are someone

only in as far as you are love,
and only what has turned to love in your life
will be preserved.

What love is
you can learn from Jesus.

He is the one who has loved most.
He will teach you to put the center of yourself
outside.
For no one has greater love
than one who dies for friends.
He will also teach you
to be unlimited space for others,
invitation and openness:
'Come to me,
all who are weary and over-burdened
and I will give you rest.'

So be converted to love every day.
Change all your energies,
all your potential,

into selfless gifts for the other person.
Then you yourself will be changed from within
and through you
God's Kingdom will break into the world.

You are called to follow Jesus closely.
With Him you will take the road
up to Jerusalem,
the city of suffering and glorification.
With Him you will give everything
that the Kingdom may come.

On this road you are called
to be least of all and not master,
to carry others' burdens
and not lay your own on them,
to give freedom instead of taking it,
to grow poor in order to make others rich,
to take the cross upon yourself
thus bringing joy to others,
to die in order that others may live.
This is the mystery of the gospel

and there is no purpose in endless talk about it.
Be silent - for it will be true and genuine
only if you practice it.

So keep Jesus Christ before your eyes.
Don't hesitate to go anywhere He leads you;
don't stay where you are and don't look back,
but look forward with eagerness
to what lies ahead.

3. Members of One Body

The community is the first place
where you will make God's kingdom incarnate.
It is one of the countless points
where God's new people assemble in peace,
in reconciliation, justice and joy,
in praise of God and service to the world.
A people whose King is the Lord.

Accept with gratitude
the companions God gives you
to go with you on the way.
Your task is to serve and upbuild one another
as members of one body.

To the extent
that you are filled with His Spirit
and ready to die that others may live,

to that extent will you grow in unity
and reflect the face of Christ
more and more clearly.

And to the extent that you are ready
to die together
that others may live
will your community bear fruit
for the coming of the Kingdom.

Then put aside all ambition,
and no longer concentrate on yourself.
Be constantly converted to your companions
and place yourself in God's hands.

Give instead of demanding,
trust others instead of compelling their trust,
serve instead of being served,
bless instead of cursing.
And be sure that when you have done
all things well
you will still be an unprofitable servant.

So be attentive to the others,
not in order to dominate or exploit them
but to work for their happiness
discreetly and effectively
and to build them up
in all the riches of faith and love.
And you, accept from your companion
the help you need.

Be thankful for the variety of gifts
and difference of personality.
When you put your own potential
and insights at the service of your community
your unity will grow stronger and richer,
and together you will create that spaciousness
which finds room for everyone.

Pluriformity is not the end
but the means to make unity more powerful
and the individual bear more fruit.

Never be satisfied with what is imperfect
yet also realise
God is patient with us.
Let progress and development
be of such a sort that all can keep pace,
and never refuse to set out together
when in obedience to the gospel
the community travels on to a new future.

Make the effort
of listening to others
and of understanding them.
Give your opinion when it is useful
without false humility
or assertiveness.
Speak in such a way
that you can still hear what the other is saying,
and that he or she will still be ready to hear you.
Whether you speak or keep silent
let it proceed from the peace of the Lord.

Take no vengeance, not even in thought.
Avoid every tendency
to depression and sadness -
it is death to your soul.
Look for the light in all things and all people.
Your night will be made radiant
by numberless stars
till the moment when the Sun of Justice
rises in your heart,
and that morning begins which knows no ending.

Your faith and love
must be constantly renewed;
your weakness and faults
constantly corrected.
Don't be afraid to open yourself
to your companions.
Choose from among them
a sure and skillful guide
who will help you advance
in the way of the Lord.

Never disappoint the trust
another puts in you.
Be warm and merciful
and let none go from you empty-handed.
The least you can offer
is your time and patience,
your affection and your prayer.

The quality of your community
does not depend on age or numbers.
The only thing that counts
and will bring you a blessing
is that you should be always seeking each other
in the Spirit of Jesus.
From Him alone comes salvation.

Have great respect
for the seniors in the community.
Don't distress them
by your talk or behavior.
Be gentle towards their weakness

and incapacities -
you are building on what they began.

Every body must have a head,
every circle a center.
Joyfully, then, accept the one
who fulfills this special service.
More than anyone else
that one needs your support and mercy.
Let the superior be for you
as a presence of the Lord,
not because of human qualities
and leadership,
but for the sake of the superior's special calling
and grace.

Everything in your life
can have love as its motive, its end.
The vows by which you bind yourself
are precisely your own way
of embodying your love for God and man.

The more you grow in love,
the more clearly you will understand
what the vows demand;
and the more seriously you live your vows,
the more you will grow in love.

4. For the Sake of the Kingdom

Your vow to remain unmarried
for the sake of God's Kingdom
will draw you into the loneliness
of the cross of Jesus
and reveal the basic loneliness
of every person.
At the same time it invites you
to build up a fellowship with Him
and to establish the kingdom of love
among all.

By not marrying you put an end
to the cycle of procreation and death.
You are beginning a new kind of existence
in the incorruptibility
of a new-born generation,

and the unimagined fruitfulness
of the Kingdom of God.

To be unmarried
does not mean for you the renouncing of love,
contempt for the body
or fear of marriage.
No, - it is the bringing of your potential for love
into the new and unlimited fruitfulness
of the Kingdom.

So you are called
to be a witness to love,
and its begetter,
an encouragement to all who are seeking
love's genuine image.

So you will also be a protest
against the narrow view
which identifies love with sex.

You will be able to do this
only if your deepest self is anchored in God,
as Jesus Himself bore witness:
I and the Father are one.
In Him you will find a love
which surpasses all human imaginings.

You will also have to be
a community person.
Make sure you don't grow isolated
from your companions on the human level.
Open yourself to the joys
of life together as family members;
foster a mature development of your feelings,
and a human warmth in your life.

Always be the first to love
and be faithful to that love
even if you get no answer.
Don't make conditions.
Be thankful and praise God
when you realize you are loved.

5. Called to Freedom

Following Jesus
demands of you in the first place
obedience to His Gospel.

You must place yourself,
alone and in community,
under the scrutiny of this Word,
and always be determining your conduct by it.
Then you will find the truth
to free you most radically,
and a solidarity
to make your community
a living gift to others.

Obedience also demands of you
that you listen to the other person;
not only to the conversation
but to what the person is.

Then you will begin to live in such a way
that you neither crush nor dominate
nor entangle your companions
but help them to be themselves
and lead them to freedom.

Christ was thus obedient
unto death
so that we might be free.
He was the least among the dead
that we might have life.
Don't be afraid then
that your obedience to the Gospel,
your listening to others,
will impoverish your personality
or decrease your responsibility.
It summons you rather
to live out your responsibility
in your encounter with others.

Never make the mistake of thinking
you can gain your freedom by

your own exertions.
It is something which you give to others
and which you receive yourself from them.

No laws, no rules,
no therapy, no discussions are capable
of setting our communities in order
and making them fruitful
if the Spirit of Jesus is not master there.

In the community there will be someone
who exercises the service of authority.
The leader's first task is to foster unity among you
and make the community grow
in faithfulness to its vocation.
The leader's authority builds up the community,
but at the same time this authority holds
only in so far as you are ready to obey.

For the full development of
each one's potentialities
a flexible yet definite structure is needed

to maintain the space
for living together.
You can't have a body without a skeleton,
or a river without banks to guide its stream.
Keep wholeheartedly to the arrangements that
have been agreed:
then people will never rely on you in vain
and you will be able to put all
your trust in others.

In obedience to each other and to the Gospel
you will discover the interior freedom
that makes you capable
of comprehending the world's needs–
without identifying in a shallow way
with special groups and causes–
and of entering into them yourself.

Our freedom is being threatened
more than ever.
Set yourself against every form
of oppression.

Free yourself from a world
that seeks only pleasures and possessions
and bring others to share your freedom.
Set yourself against everything
that makes us slaves
politically, economically, socially.
You have nothing to lose.

No doubt you will have noticed
that our fundamental bondage
is to sin,
to our short-sighted attachment to ourselves.

Through your radical surrender to God
you will be freed from this
and become a deliverer of others.
a breath of fresh air for those you meet,
a servant of all,
a source of life, expectation and hope.

6. That We Might Be Rich

You are ready to put all you have
at the service of others.
You seek poverty not for its own sake,
nor from contempt or fear
for the good things God gives you,
but because you want to contribute something
to alleviate the world's poverty,
to make even your own possessions available.

Remember the words of Paul:
'You know the grace of our Lord Jesus Christ,
that though he was rich,
yet for your sake he became poor,
so that by his poverty you might become rich.'

The community is the place
where you daily share

riches and poverty,
energy and weakness,
joy and sorrow,
success and failure,
your hope and your doubt.
In this kind of community can grow
something of Christ's bond with His Father:
'All that I have is yours,
all that you have is mine.'

Live like a poor person
without parading your poverty.
Stand by the poor wherever they live and work.
Your first love must go out
to the least of these.
Don't tie yourself down to the rich or powerful
of the world.
Get rid of the inclination
to court the great and influential.
Otherwise you would deform
the image of the Church.

Put your trust in God,
wait for His mercy
and for all that you need.
Above all, take Jesus as your riches,
the pearl for which you will give everything,
your treasure in heaven.

Don't be romantic about this;
take your part in the simple struggle for a living,
but without attaching your heart
to what you earn by it.
In this way you will be able to help many people
and at the same time be a condemnation
of every form of materialism or snobbery.

Don't suppose poverty
consists only in big things.
Keep clear of all competitiveness and envy;
treat with care the things we
possess in common.
Be sober and restrained,
and don't wait till you are asked outright

before giving anything.
But don't suppose poverty
consists only in little things.
Share with the whole world.
A generous contribution to relieve poverty
is better than a little gift;
and an intelligent and effective effort
to fight the causes of poverty
is better than almsgiving.

Keep in mind also
how much you lack yourself;
be aware of your own poverty
and dare to hold out your hands
to receive from others
and to learn from them.

7. The Breaking of the Bread

By the grace of God
you have been called to a life
in which everything is inspired
by the sacrament of the Eucharist.
You must grow in daily knowledge
of this mystery,
and in a greater love for the Lord
who gives Himself in it.

The celebration of the Eucharist
is the centre of your life.
It is the highest expression
and the strongest support
of your life in community.
It is the beginning and end of your actions;
the source and consummation
of your service to God.

When you celebrate the memorial of Christ
give thanks to God
for His countless benefits.
Never tire of praising Him
one in heart and voice with your companions,
and united with Christ, the sacrifice of praise.
Renew yourself in the spirit of love and unity
because you are sharing with your friends,
the same bread, the same cup.

The celebration of the Eucharist
would be nothing but a romantic
or aesthetic sensation
should you forget
that the heart of it
is the self-giving of Jesus.
The sacrifice of yourself for the sake of the others
is the single foundation of every community.
Unite yourself with the Lord, then,
in a fruitful and acceptable offering
for the life of the world.

Each day you are nourished at the Lord's table
and filled with His riches.
So be ready to break
the bread of your life
for the poor and hungry everywhere
in the world.
Keep nothing for yourself
but share with the others
all you have received from God's tenderness.

In the bread of the Eucharist
and the cup of blessing
Christ's presence is revealed
at its most intense.
Let your life be permeated
with a tremendous reverence
towards this mystery of faith.
Your adoration needs no justification
more than your love and wonder
for the infinite, delicate grandeur of God,
the unfathomable depths of Christ's gift.
Let His praise not depart from your lips.

Life drawn from the Eucharist
makes all kinds of demands on you
to proclaim the meaning and greatness
of this mystery.

You are called especially
to give the sacrament its full effect
in unity, love and service.
The unity of all Christians
and all persons in the world
must be closest to your heart.
Always and everywhere you are called
to rise above oppositions and divisions
in the universal love of Christ.
Always look for what unites
and fight everything that
estranges and separates
us from one another.

Your calling gives you the privilege
of living the eucharistic mystery to the full.
So reject nothing which the church

enjoins on your faith,
and accept nothing that might obscure
the full meaning of this sacrament.

To Christ the Lord
who dwells ever present in His gifts
you can bring your life's adoration.

Your whole life must be worship
in spirit and truth,
your whole existence a celebration
and adoration of the presence of God.
Your life is to be poured out
in prayer and adoration
before the Eucharist,
and there it will be inspired afresh.
In this way give glory to the Father
through Him, in Him and with Him.

The Eucharist sets you on the way of Christ.
it takes you into His redeeming death
and gives you a share

in the most radical deliverance possible.
And already the light of the resurrection,
the new creation,
is streaming through it from beyond.
Whenever you sit at table with the risen Lord,
it is the first day of the week,
very early in the morning.

8. Prayer

The Lord Jesus Himself will teach you
how you should pray.
He is the creative Word
which you may receive in the
silence of your heart
and the fruitful soil of your life.
Listen attentively to what He will say;
be swift to carry out
what He will ask of you.
You have been promised His Spirit
who will bear your poor little efforts
before the throne of grace
and into the intimacy of the living God.

Your prayer is therefore not so much a duty
as a privilege;
a gift rather than a problem
or the result of your own efforts.

So don't tire yourself out
looking for beautiful thoughts or words,
but stay attentive before God
in humility and expectation,
in desire and purity of heart,
full of joy and hope.
Your prayer will take countless forms
because it is the echo of your life,
and a reflection of the inexhaustible light
in which God dwells.

Sometimes you will taste and see how good
the Lord is.
Be glad then, and give Him all honour,
because His goodness to you has no measure.
Sometimes you will be dry and joyless
like parched land or an empty well.
But your thirst and helplessness
will be your best prayer
if you accept them with patience
and embrace them lovingly.

Sometimes your prayer will be an experience
of the infinite distance that separates
you from God;
sometimes your being and His fullness
will flow into each other.

Sometimes you will be able to pray
only with your body and hands and eyes;
sometimes your prayer will move beyond
words and images;
sometimes you will be able to leave
everything behind you
to concentrate on God and His Word.
Sometimes you will be able to do nothing else
but take your whole life and everything in you
and bring them before God.
Every hour has its own possibilities
of genuine prayer.

Don't be afraid to set apart
a considerable time for your prayer every day.
It is your vocation.

Your zeal for the Kingdom of God
and your availability for all your companions
will grow all the greater for it.
Remember that prayer is more powerful
than anything you can achieve by your actions.
And the Lord says there are evils
that can only be cast out
by prayer and fasting.

So set yourself again and again
on the way of prayer.
Never wait till you feel the need for it.
Often enough, if you only make a new start,
God will bring it to a good end.
Make use of a method when you need it.
Learn from your companions
and study how the saints of God have prayed.

As you pray in community
you will discover the wide horizon
of each prayer.
Rejoice to meet your companions

in the presence of the Lord,
and to look with them to the Father of all light.
Let yourself be carried by the rhythm of prayer
in the peace and joy of a new world.
Let yourself be healed of the wounds
you suffer every day
by the saving praise of God.

Let yourself be renewed
in your faith, hope and love
by the Word that comes to you.
Don't let yourself be distracted by accidentals.
Try to understand God's Word
even in the mouth of a bad reader.
Don't be irritated
by the one who sings off-key.
The forms are only important to the extent
that you know how to see through them.

Don't pray so that the world may admire you,
nor to draw others eyes.
Pray so that God may be glorified

and His name praised.
Unite yourself with the unceasing prayer
of the church on earth and in heaven.
Know that through your mouth and heart
all of creation is proclaiming the glory of God
and groaning for its redemption in the Lord.

In this way your life will be fed with prayer
and full of this search for God.
You will be able to give without
counting the cost,
and accomplish God's will every day.
You will dedicate yourself heart and soul
to the battle against the powers of evil
and you will work
with joy and indestructible hope
for the new humanity
for which Jesus gave His life and blood.
Prayer and work
are not whole without each other.

9. The Harvest is Great

Your first task
is to co-operate in the building
of a loving community.
This is the condition and effect
of what we celebrate in the Eucharist.
In your community
begins the reality of the new humanity
in which the complex fragmentation
of our human existence and society of life
is healed and sanctified.

Your community does not exist for itself.
If it is truly evangelical
it will guide you and free you
to serve the people of God.
It is itself an active element
in realising the Kingdom.

God will urge you to go out from the community
to give form to His message of reconciliation
and unity among all.
Through the suffering and joy
of all whom you will encounter
you will let all your daily experience
reverberate through your prayer,
alone and with your companions.

You have been called to be in the world
without being of the world.
If the salt loses its savour
it is good for nothing.
Therefore don't reject the world
and don't cut yourself off from people,
but love them as Jesus, the Redeemer, did.

But where the world
is nothing but the pride of life,
lust of the eyes, and desire of the flesh,
then flight alone is proper.

If you were to value this world
you could not be God's friend.

Your only ambition must be
to proclaim in word and deed
Christ's gospel of freedom,
justice and love.
For this use the most effective means
without supposing that they can
replace God's grace.

You are free to do the work you want to do.
You can live as a religious and be a
witness to the Lord
in every kind of work.
Discover for yourself
what seems the most fruitful field for you.
Be enterprising and creative.
God blesses the risks
undertaken for His sake.

When you choose your work be influenced
by its consequences for your life in community
and by the needs of the local church.
Preferably look for work
that you can do to the greatest benefit
of the community
and in which it can support you most effectively.

Therefore always consult others.
You will thus prevent unnecessary conflicts
and avoid seeking yourself
or losing sight of your goal.

You are never alone in your work.
You can profit by the insights,
knowledge, experience and contacts
of your companions.
Be involved yourself with the whole group
and take interest in the work of others;
offer them your help where you can.

The love of Christ will not let you rest.
Your work is no escape into activity,
but a sharing in the upbuilding
of the body of Christ.
You can do this only on the basis
of an intimate union with Him
in purity of heart and selflessness.

It is not necessary to do your work
within a tight schedule
or the structure of a labour contract.
The community gives you the precious possibility
of committing yourself freely,
and developing your own initiatives
for the good of God's Kingdom.

If you think you are called
to the diaconate or priesthood
you are striving for something good.
See it as a high election,
a responsible mission.
It will be your task

to lead and instruct your people in the name
of the Lord,
to sanctify and upbuild them in the Spirit.
This demands an obedient union with the bishop
and a collegial union with the other priests.

If you are called to the diaconate or priesthood,
it will mean a new call to holiness
and love for the Lord and His people.

10. The Body of the Lord

The way of Jesus
leads to communion with all people.
His enduring presence in the Church
is the foundation of a profound community
in the world
just as God desires it.

Love the Church as the Lord Himself.
Though she is burdened with the weakness
and sinfulness of a long history
she is still the instrument of His Kingdom,
His work of salvation for the world,
the germ of a new creation.

Show solidarity with all your brothers
and sisters in the faith.
One baptism and the same Eucharist

are the visible signs of your unity.
Be specially mindful of those
who are being persecuted by the world
for the sake of faith and righteousness.

Your love for the Church will also be expressed
in a union of faith with the Holy Father.
He fulfils a mission of unifying
and upbuilding for the whole Church.
Every fracture in the body
means a mutual impoverishment,
and conflicts with the will of the Lord.

If you love the Church
have a profound respect for her institutions
and mission.
Whatever is impure and useless in her
must be healed, not attacked,
and purified in suffering rather than criticised.

Give yourself time to discover this Church
as a marvellously deep mystery

of fellowship in faith, hope and love,
transcending all barriers of time and space.
Built upon the foundation of the apostles
and prophets,
she makes you members of the household
of all God's saints.

The Church comes into being
in the community where you live,
not so much in her official structures
as in her essential form of brotherhood
and new creation.

Remember then that your community
must before all else be one and holy,
catholic and apostolic.
In this way you will live the mystery
of the Church
in the place where you are.

11. The Spiritual Life

Spiritual life
is life drawn from the Holy Spirit,
who raised Jesus from the dead
and turns the whole world into a new creation.

The Spirit within you
will bear fruit
of simplicity and goodness,
modesty and joy,
sobriety and gentleness.
He will give you interior freedom
and bring your love to perfection.
He will make you into a new person.

So don't carry on a futile battle against yourself,
don't divide yourself into good and evil.
Resist the temptation to analyse yourself–
turn your attention to the Lord instead,

and be deeply receptive.
Accept yourself in His light
and concentrate on the mission
you have to accomplish.

God's Spirit will bring you to simplicity
in an undivided dedication
to Him and to your neighbors.
He gives you no programme
but the chance of turning yourself towards love
hour by hour.
And so spiritual life is not a burden
but a liberating vocation.
It is much more a matter of simplifying
than of complicated methods
and extraordinary performances.

In special cases it can be good
to impose some specific discipline on yourself.
Your daily life among your companions
and others
in service, openness and fidelity

is the usual form of ascesis,
which is both effective and enough.

Every day look at the way you are living
in the light of God's Word.
Let it warm you when you are cold,
encourage you when you are disappointed.
You must not only be a hearer of the Word—
you must also bring it to fulfilment.
Happy are you if you meditate upon it
daily in your heart:
you will be like a tree by the running water,
whose branches will stay fresh and green,
and they will keep bringing forth new fruit.

Spiritual life will develop
only in a climate of silence.
Bring the warring voices within you to stillness.
Create an atmosphere of tranquillity and silence
with your companions,
and so help each other to remain
concentrated on the presence of God.

It is also a sign of respect
for your friends who are studying,
praying or resting.

You will surely have realised
that you cannot become a spiritual person
without an interior discipline
in your dealings with the world.
Don't let yourself be trapped into the unrest
that comes from excessive talking
and gossiping.

Be discerning in your choice
of what the television, radio and
papers offer you.
Without a personal control
on your imagination and emotions
you will undermine your spiritual strength
and lessen your chances
of genuinely meeting and loving one another.

You will find a source of wisdom
and spiritual joy in the feasts of the Church.
The year is crowned with the signs
of God's goodness.
If you celebrate these feasts with the Church
then your own life and suffering,
your enthusiasm and work,
your dying and rising
and your waiting for the Lord
will receive significance and impact.

Never be misled by the thought
that after failing and sinning
there can be no forgiveness.
Look critically at your own shortcomings,
but be sure that with the Lord
there is always abundance of redemption.

Your spiritual life must be mobile;
travel from oasis to oasis.
Yet the Lord can prepare a table

even in the desert,
and in the furnace of trial
He will be coolness and refreshment.

12. Mary

Mary will have her own place in your life.
You cannot separate her from the Lord
who chose her as His mother and His bride.

She is the selfless space
where God became man;
she is the silence in which God's Word
can be heard.
She is the free woman, subject to none,
not even to the powers of evil.

She is the image of the Church.
Her self-effacing service will guide you
to the Lord.
Her faith and fidelity
are a model for your life.

She has trodden all the paths
of our human existence;

she has gone through darkness and suffering,
through the abyss of loneliness and pain.

She is the little creature
through whom God's grandeur shines out;
she is the poor one
filled with divine riches.
She is wholly grace,
and grace for you.

Then take your part joyfully
in the prophecy of scripture:
'Behold, henceforth all generations
will call me blessed.'

13. Of Days and Years

Your life unfolds
in a continuous succession
of experiences and expectations.
No two days are the same,
no year leaves you unaltered.

Every day has enough trouble of its own.
When you go to sleep,
bury all that has happened in the mercy of God.
It will be safe there.
Stand back from what has happened,
and be grateful for it all.

When the day begins
be sure that you yourself can be
as new and pure as the new light.
It is like a resurrection.

The first hour is the most important of the day.
Don't yield to laziness,
but greet with joy
the new opportunities God offers you.

Even in the complicated world of today
try to keep close to a natural rhythm of life.
Meals taken together
should be moments of rest in your day.
See your encounters with others
as high peaks in your life,
and upbuilding.

The evenings are particularly suited
for talking and companionship,
joy and relaxation.
But here too the more you give
the more you will receive.
Be careful
not to prolong your evenings indefinitely.
In the long run it will produce nothing good.
If you are visiting friends,

don't keep them away from their rest
but know how to end your visit at a decent hour.

Your way through life
will not remain the same.
There are years of happiness and years
of suffering.
There are years of abundance,
and years of poverty,
years of hope, and of disappointment,
of building up, and of breaking down.
But God has a firm hold on you
through everything.

There are years of strength
and years of weakness,
years of certainty, years of doubt.
It is all part of life,
and it is worth the effort
to live it to the end
and not give up before it is accomplished.

You need never stop growing.
A new future is always possible.
Even on the other side of death
a new existence waits for you
in the fulness of that glory
which God has prepared for you
from the beginning.

14. The End and the Beginning

This rule is not meant to be a burden for you.
Nor does it pretend to be complete.
It should help you discover and experience
how great is the freedom to which
you are called,
and how great the responsibility
which you may take upon yourself.
Be so faithful to this rule today
that you can be faithful again tomorrow.

Set out on the road together with
your companions,
together with the numberless people of God,
all pilgrims travelling to the Father's house.
Go on your way singing,
a song of hope on your lips
and your heart burning within you.

Now we have the alleluias of the journey,
soon there will be the alleluias of consummation,
of the great sabbath with God.

Now you are being sown
in the darkness of the earth;
when that day comes, you will bloom
in the light and warmth of God's eternity.

Set out on the road,
and peace be with you
for ever.